LOOK U

Look up without Laughing

Robert Havard

First Impression—1998

ISBN 1 85902 651 6

This volume is published with the support of the Arts Council of Wales.

Printed in Wales at
Gomer Press, Llandysul, Ceredigion, Wales

For my daughters
Lucy and Hannah

CONTENTS

I

Shadow

Corrugating down
steep slopes and sidings
one autumn evening
the ferns cut deep brown.
The pit below drowned
in silence without
wheel crank, dram or shout.
Shadow of a man
walking on the land
he knows inside out.

Collier's Song

Burn me with the coal
sang the collier,
I won't have my bones in a shroud.
Burn me with the coal
sang the collier,
I won't lie in a box underground.

Let my ashes rise in smoke
he sang,
let my ashes rise in a cloud.
I won't lie in a box underground
sang the collier,
I won't have my bones in a shroud.

Burn me with the coal.
Burn me with the coal.
I won't have my bones in a shroud
sang the collier,
I won't lie in a box underground.

Rhondda Farewell [1960]

There are three hairpins on the mountain road
and three slat benches where old miners sit
counting cars and staring across the rows
of slate at the pocks of slag opposite.
On the highest the talk is pigeons, squabs,
allotments, the majority of them fit,
smoothing trouser legs and coughing up gobs
of phlegm to slake their throat. Down a bit
there's less to say: packed in tight as a wad
of twist, they scrutinize each other's spit,
sucking hard on air as the thin fags trod
underfoot. On the last bench, by the pit,
chin to a scarf above the acts of God,
one tries to wave, if that's what you'd call it.

Green Ballad [1965]

The MG dug its wheels in dirt
and parked below a horseshoe bend
where old miners sat slaking twist
to keep their throat saliva wet.
Two smart guys got out quick and crossed
to see the view, while on the bench
they chomped on dull as Barbary apes
wondering what was picturesque
about a mountain charred in slag
that fetched two blokes in like them
who do half Europe in a week
cameras slung around their neck.

That quiet it was no one heard
what the tall bloke in denim said,
pointing at the mountain opposite
and shaking out his locks of hair.
The other bloke was adamant though
and brandishing a map to check
their lie he scratched it on his nail
and laughed as if he'd won a bet.
The old timers sat and watched bemused
by maps and telescopic lens
but what they couldn't fathom was
while blond locks looked on unimpressed
his fat mate fell about each time
he marked his atlas with an X.

When they finished and turned to go
they saw their audience on the bench,
gaping hard with all gums chomping
and sucking mountain air like eggs.
Half in the car but still half out
the denim bloke froze, his unkempt
hair like Porthcawl surf, all chopped up
in the wind: 'Scandalous', he said.
'Ought never been allowed. Give us
five years you won't know yourself.
That mountain will be full of trees,
this grass will all be green again'.

Two doors slammed and they were gone
for neither had much Barbary Welsh.
But as they charged off up the hill
their chrome hung souvenirs of phlegm.

Epitaphs [1975]

They kept their word about the trees.
All tidy, regimental pines.
Each one, in the vast cemeteries,
salutes an unknown of the mines.

The Roadman

Tea slops warm in his belly
as he leaves his shed and walks into the mist
that spills in slow motion
from the forestry pines.
Two hours booting stones at the verge
overlooking the village
on his gamey leg. Longer
if ice squirts rock like lambs from an ewe
or snow tucks in at the bends.
January. No time to loll,
binoculars handy, and roll a fat fag.
No time to watch a peregrine feeding,
eyes agog on its buttress ledge.
January was all go and the grass was wet anyway.
He might have to unblock a culvert,
pull a tree or carcass from a cwm's hole,
water filling round him like a bath.
He might have to phone down the yard
emergency, brew up for the gang who'd come in
heave-ho to dry their arse at his stove.
January. Only the road, the stones
and the rain that ran down ancient grooves of rock
that spoke of sin and salvation.
Only the mist and the sudden headlamps of cars
to shake a big fist at.

What did they know
about the lives he'd saved? What did they know
about stones, landslips, subsidence
that buried a man's bones without trace?

All they knew was their precious jobs in asbestos
tents on the other side, the years on their Mazdas
ringed in rust. They couldn't read rock,
calligraphy, hieroglyphics,
loud and legible to him as ELVIS LIVES,
history beneath the trash evangelical paint.
But one day he'd show them as he'd once shown me
his explorations, excavations,
Egyptological Discoveries on Rhigos Mountain:
A Treatise written in immaculate copper plate
except the lines went up a bit to the right and almost
off the page like a man limping into the mist.

Gwilym Trefleming

With nearly a twelvemonth
for every lump of dust
you sat quiet in your corner
deaf to the rest of us.
The grate always handy
for your pint and smokes,
with Trevor sipping ready
to bus you up the slopes.

The night Burton came in
—introductions all round—
no one thought you, Gwilym,
had heard a bloody sound.
But the rugby fizzled out,
the fire spat, made a hiss,
when you said 'Mr Jenkins,
why pay taxes to them Swiss?'

That night in the snug
we got a pint apiece,
but the fullest looking one
was on the mantelpiece.

George Sailor

I saw you in the polo photo,
muscles like a tree,
water polo that was,
shot in '33.
You must have loved the water
George,
or had fear of the dark,
for one night when the lights went out
you ran away to sea.

They say the sherry got you,
too much Cutty Sark,
when it came to sailing
you didn't need an ark.
I saw your post-war blackouts
George,
legless here sometimes,
but what I saw in your crazy eyes
was fear of the dark.

Tom Picton, mountain-fighter [1895-1939]

Tom Picton, why d'you go to Spain,
some bastard get you drunk again?

Was in the Railway Bar,
never knew his name.
Said he'd see me in Espanya,
put me on the Cardiff train.

Tom Picton, why d'you go to Spain,
you punchy now, got clots on the brain?

Had my fill of punching holes
in butties on the mountain,
a gutsful of picking coals
now Maudie's gone again.

Tom Picton, why d'you go to Spain,
think you'll stand a bullet's pain?

Can always duck and bend
see boy. Only bullet
that can kill me, friend,
has got my name on it.

Tom Picton, Twmmy boy, why d'you go to Spain?

—For Christsake, mun, I came.

Paranoia Classroom: Penyrenglyn

Even when he had stormed their minds
to silence and each boy shook apart
in Atlantic isolation
—Bailey, Malin, Rockall, Faeroes—
there was no respite for him,
no easing of the noise that scratched
his brain.
                    Even as he watched them sit,
eyes blank on a tedious page,
he saw their minds shift to other things
—Viking, Dogger, Cromarty, German Bight—
and when his chalk drew near the slate
he heard a pen fall from a dull hand
to the notched floor and the oil-less
cranking of wood on metal from mutilated
desks.
                    Even as they froze in awkward
prayer and he prided himself on what he wasn't
—winder, haulier, checkweigher, collier—
each fidget magnified in his brain
like mental arithmetic and there was no
—Lundy, Fasnet, Sole, Irish Sea—
respite from the unambiguous smells,
from the panes that filled like stamp albums
—Magyar, Helvetia, Deutschland, Danmark—
full of mountain, leaning on the school,
flat, on the class —Biscay, Finisterre,
Sole, Southeast Iceland— heavy as the minutes
of hands that jerked the promotions
he shared with them and the electric clock.

Evocation of Rhondda

Rhondda.
Not the Hollywood schmaltz of black and white minstrels.
Not the venerable documentary soaked in statistics.
Not the Rhondda cherished by lugubrious painters:
    slanting rain, slate and slag.
Not even the Rhondda I grew to love
    on tales of Spain and Revolution.
But a Rhondda with no history, no literature, no art.
    Rhondda pure and simple.
    The Rhondda of my childhood.

Taff Street where we played against the Council gates
    and someone always scooped the ball too high
so Dai Shivers had to throw it back shouting:
    'Next time I'll put a knife through it!'
Dai had a deep voice and a scowl and he walked with a limp
    so we always believed him.
But the only balls that didn't come back
    went over the railings into the river.
[They must have had netfuls of balls in Porth.]

Taff Street where the girls skipped in the middle of the road
    plastered in hopscotch:

    'On a mountain
    stands a lady,
    who she is
    I do not know.
    She is dressed in
    gold and silver
    waiting for
    a nice young beau'.

And the boys, when they weren't chopping trees for bonfires,
    marched up and down with locked arms singing:

'Three jolly Welshmen
looking for a job . . .'

There were lots of jobs, to be had then
            and lots of gold and silver marriages.

At three in the afternoon Vic Basini walked across the bridge
to the Con Club with his white ice-cream apron wrapped tight round him
and at half-past four he walked back with his apron flapping loose
            arguing in broken English with Garnet Davies
            who spoke real Welsh and made coffins in a shed
            between the river and the siding.

Garnet had a sister with tangled hair who was mad we called Scatty
            who stalked the *gwli* from her house to the shed
            jumping at shadows and making shadows jump.

            'Scatty! Scatty! Scatty!'
            we shouted to make her throw stones.
            'Scatty! Scatty! Scatty!'
            to make her tear her hair.

            But no one went down that *gwli* alone
            and even in a gang we ran full-pelt.
            [We thought she slept at night in a coffin.]

One afternoon between two sheds backing onto the river
            I saw a brownhaired girl lift her skirt to squat.
She looked up and her eyes that were round and dark as nuts were smiling
            and my head rushed away with the river.

            Ycha fi! Ycha fi!
I heard the sirens wake the miners before dawn.
            Ycha fi! Ycha fi!
There was a commotion of flooding in one of the pits.

21

But I never went up the mountain to chop trees
            for the bonfire again.
Only with a brownhaired girl who had nuts for eyes
            who liked to lie in the ferns,
a girl who wiped coal off the seats on the school bus
            before she sat down.

It was behind one of the siding sheds I had my first smoke,
sitting on stones which I nearly fell off into the river.
We did a lot of things there for the first time
            and some for the last.

Taff Street with its clouds of smoke from the railway
and wagon after wagon of coal rumbling off to Cardiff.
            I never thought they would ever stop rumbling.
And the majorettes and marching bands blowing their bazookas.
            I never thought they would ever stop marching
or that miners wouldn't walk on the mountain on Sundays
            with kids clinging to their backs
            blinking in the sun and shouting.

            Cwm Saerbren
                        Penyrenglyn
                                    Ynyswen.

The words came out in a sort of Welsh,
the mongrel Welsh of Rhondda,
a soft sing-song that was neither English nor Welsh
but only what the people spoke,
            eyes laughing or running with tears.

Rhondda.
Taff Street.
Where I could almost touch the ferns on the mountain.
Where the farm's glow at night was as high as a star.
That I left one day like a ball bobbing on the river.

Magic Mountain: Tynewydd

The mountain in the middle of the street
did not obstruct traffic, spoil children's games
or disturb the flop-eared dreams of dachshunds
who dozed in summer on its sunlit skirts.
The mountain in the middle of the street
had gone unnoticed for generations,
not troubling draught mares, Sturmey Archer gears
on delivery bikes, or making trams shudder
with undue precipitation. In fact,
the mountain in the middle of the street
was only in the middle of the street
a split second, going up Gwendoline
swinging into Wyndham. And only then
at dawn when birds took their first deep June breath.

Royal Visit

The station festooned: bunting, red carpet,
dais, potted palms. The brewery tricoloured,
draping Lady Margaret's charnel wheels.
The piled wagons shunted to discreet sidings,
the charred stacks banked to let the air breathe.
A hill of faces winged in white collars,
rows of brass and the choir's diamond baton
aloft, poised to perforate the tumbling mist.
He, classic coat, naval beard and bowler,
skips down to a quarterdeck. She, high laced
and unhurried, barely lifts her brocade,
smiling wisely. Pause. He scours the thin sky
for bearings—panic [cough] and penance [cough]—,
turns on Stamfordham: [Where the fuck are we?]

Treherbert, 12.30 pm, Thursday 27 June 1912.

Rhymes

With a net in my hand
I saw the river
quiver with fish.
With a cake in my hand
I saw the sun
run to its oven hill.
With a torch in my hand
I saw the moon
zoom on a sheep's skull.
Torch, cake, net:
my hand
cold, burnt, wet.

★

River
don't you know
it's
rude to go
as soon as you've come in,
especially when the
snow
sits
so
comfy on the mountain?

★

If it weren't for the sky
that comes sometimes with its snow
and I saw first one morning
close by my bedroom window,
how was I going to know
the mountain has other sides
where its other rivers flow?

★

The sun sets on mountain
lovelier than the sea,
its glow on still rock falls
more heavy than waves gleam,
with shroud lights billowing
as the hill shoulders heave
a sky of autumn fern
turns black as three-foot seams.

Look up without Laughing

Between the ruins of mountain
hysterectomized in scars
the sky is a bizarre blue.
High above the potash swell
the sun cleaves from the tip's dry
nipple, her fern cut shadows dyed
down the arrowed dimples of grass.
Watch her climb the funicular sky
—manjacked on a gold ratchet—
blinking bride, this Disney morning.

Loud as the lines of washing,
overtures of the icecream van,
a dog's bark rising, stubs
of irredeemable boys stamp
out of doors with the cooking
sounds like clear spirals of noise
up the choral mountain's spine.
In Samaritan laybyes
sheep eat the cool grass silent
and dream of Merlin's cabbages
open-eyed.

          Down the pigeonlofts
and the thermosflask allotments
by the cardboard river bank
mouse minis race blood red
past swimming-pool blue, bowling-green
green, house leans on house in slate
concertinas, touch and go
the train jet speeds injections
up the valley's sunburnt vein
and a whistle rips the sunlight
like a varicose rainbow
in the blue Sleeping Beauty air.

'Though this is where I was born
this is not where I shall die',
says a fat man on the platform:
'Three and seven, we're off to Devon.
Top of the shop, London next stop'.
And when the diesel door slams
shut the engine trips back down
with the river, sensitive as eggs
to subsidence and wormy skulls
whiter than Majorcan bellies.

'Three jolly Welshmen
looking for a job'
sing the boys on the siding.

'What kind of job?'
asks a voice in Cwm Saerbren.

'A better job than you can do
any day',
Tynewydd lads say.

'Show us then',
shouts Ynyswen.

Still the chimneys smoke regardless
like those girls from Penyrenglyn
when a bride fills Libanus porch
a minute and confetti falls
like guano, wet as Mondays,
on a gorsedd of patent bags.
Her teeth freeze weddingcake white
and photo-finish in the hard light
as seven dwarfs unpick the pennies
that usher her to her limousine
to sit her collection plates down.

Uneasy in the eyesore sun
in a canyon grand and ugly
where roof and horizon touch
tuberculously loving,
the last day-shift comes ashore
on cue in one amphibious host.
Faces clowned in charcoal etchings
leave their cage in iron silence
never having seen How Green
Was My Valley obviously.

'This man winds his wires out,
wires out . . .'

'Aye, spiders down the spout.'

'This man digs like a mole,
like a mole . . .'

'Aye, up your big black hole!'

'And this man drives in anthracite,
anthracite . . .'

'Aye, where flowers bloom at night.'

On baize the cue ball crosses baulk
and bright constellations spin,
fall in their nets like atomic
fishes when a man whose skull
is whiter than a Majorcan belly
comes up into the still shining sun
that sweats the blue vein of his nose:

'Can't we have our jobs then?'
cry the boys on Cwm Saerbren.

'Not until you're grown men',
the shout comes back from Ynyswen.

'But we've got to earn our living',
sob the boys on the siding.

'The time for that is long gone',
says a distant voice in Ton.

Unanimous hands go up
as the black flops into its net
one last time this afternoon.
And it must be getting on too
for the fat man wonders if
it's nostalgia he feels
changing trains at Cardiff,
will he miss his Arms Park seat,
the sea of red right to the pitch
singing their anthem for him,
the guilt when they boo the queen?

Only when he's far far away
—wrapped in a *Wales on Wednesday*
fanzine and nearly dislexic
on microchips— does it grab him
like a vindaloo by the throat:
Kingdom Koal, funicularize it
job-lot without telling a soul, fern
to ferris-wheel in five minutes flat,
Cherokee wigwams and a Dragon
Theme-Park thrown in, checkweights each end,
the *Jolly Collier* serving dark:

> '*Bara* when I'm hungry,
> *cwrw* when I'm dry,
> *gwely* when I'm tired
> and *nefoedd* when I die'.

30

Aye, as any black and white
minstrel will tell you any night,
if it's not *nefoedd* it's nirvana
they'll be after after happy hour,
speeds your journey
twice as fast as lager, sunshine,
takes away the appetite.

You can tell the night is drawing in
for the boys have stopped chasing goals
long ago on Bute mountain
where bonfires stacked like telegraph
poles and hand to mouth Woodbines
went round and round till the sun
ran oven dark behind the loud hill
and the jam-fingered evening called them
all in as the light fell yellow in gas
and Welshcake shadows crumbled in sleep.

    'Oh those elves, elves,
    the devil's elves,
    why can't they stay themselves?'

Shush now, love, much wickeder
thoughts come out to play at night
in the loins of the darkest *twch*.
It's very sad, Marquis de Sade
when all you want is a burning bush.

In Chrichton Street the wallpaper
makes its petals squeeze an old man's chest
and over the last scars of light
a curtain draws like stitches
through the cool Sleeping Beauty air
sowing lovebites in the laybyes.
Weightless the empty glasses crack
under bellies of men singing
snug out of their railwayman's club:

31

'Rock of ages
pound a pound,
earnt my wages
underground'.

All the way home they sing, the rust
of railings on their shoulder,
the night's finger down their throat
spicing with dust and vinegar
what can be saved from the street:

'There was no pollution,
no soiling of the grass,
only absolution
for the working class'.

And before long, certainly long
before their eiderdowns are thick
as a song of snores, all the soft white
roses will have closed down for the night.

The Valley

The valley is a knife.
I was cut in the valley.
The valley is an empty coal gut.
I was born in the womb of the valley.
The valley is vertical demolition.
I was razed to the ground in the valley.
The valley is a thousand foot grave.
I must not be buried in the valley.
I must get out of the valley to breathe.
I must get out of the valley to see.
I must climb out
I must break out
I must leave
the valley
the valley
the valley.

II

Bottle of Stout

Heavy stout, rich, bubbling stout,
champing at the open neck,
eager in black roots, forcing
along the neck, rich in foam,
so fast, so rich, exploding
in honeyed cox-combs and black
once more asleep in the glass.

Dummy

See the dummy, her plastic skin
pinked in glass, fix her neutral eye
on minds sucked numb and smell out gin
in sentimental passers-by.
Unreal she'll pose like a photo
and point modestly to Soho.
Under horns and lights the concrete
cuts open to a pneumatic drill.
Naked in her silent idyll
she'll guard her breast that's lost its teat.

Venice USA

for Lowell

A small room scratched out of odd
timbers washed up on the beach.
The moonlight lopes its way in,
bright, ebony, showing each
cigarette burn, old coffee ring
and the torn cover of Nietzsche.
He lives, or refuses to,
here against the dollar's siege:
monastic adolescence,
though one day he'll have to teach.

Portugal

[Lisboa]

Lisboa,
smooth as a woman's leg,
delicate.

Lisboa,
tall houses in white
and pale, pale red
that fade into the sky
unnoticed.

Lisboa,
pale as old jeans,
a Dufy painting
with lines, long lines
of sunlight and sail.

Lisboa,
framed in a woman's limbs
stretching.

[Portimão]

Empty streets gape into the sun
and wide squares
must be crossed before the shade.

The shade hangs perpendicular
from an eave
cutting the street like Sagres cliff
black and white.

Fish and salt sting one's lips
and a nag
with carnival plumes and a carriage
stamps the cobble.

A swarthy man leaves the tavern,
his throat cracking
like the fancy whip in his hand.

[Sagres]

Sagres,
wind and surf
and the caw of an ancient gull.

Sagres,
the wind bleak,
sharp as the cliff,
true as a compass.

Sagres,
a dead bird falls
and an oar floats
on the horizon.

Sagres,
wind and surf
and the caw of an ancient gull.

Santiago

[Cathedral]

'Light!
Light of our lives!'
the robed voice bellowed.
'Light!
Light first born
in a stable poor!'
shouted down old doubts,
heckled our silence,
shawl devils,
stone.

And light, light
resounded in arches
massive with shadow,
radiant as the altar's
candle gold;
that ancient voice,
its microphone:
'Light, light, light . . !'
But there were many arches,
many draughts.
I left cold.

[Rosalía]

Outside
your shadows spike
like a crown of thorns.
Too pat
the damp streets mourn.
By the same cold hands
this bread I bought
was sold to pilgrims
years ago
and time is a grain of corn
cobbled in a beggar's palm.

Though it was not of them,
if you welcomed them,
but of a girl you turned away
I thought.
She faces you still,
head slung down,
a birthmark speared in her heart.
Yes,
this is the town
where bones are brought.

Old Woman and Sundial

In Mijas, on its granite strata,
facing the Mediterranean
and the limpid sands of Africa,
I saw her, sitting in the sun.
Bent in an arch at the Roman
dial, she broke crusts on her knees;
her fissured hands cast a frieze
of shadow, pecked by doves. Wobegone
she mourned the cold: 'My sons all gone
Lord, to Málaga, the Germanies'.

Machismo at Nerja

Blue: tension of sea
and sky.
Hard yellow rock
extends a thirst
even to the vibrant parallel.
A blade hangs
brutal and silver
over the greenless.
It would cut a piece of chocolate flesh
and quench this salt.

The Phenomenology of Don Jorge

In memory of Jorge Guillén

The book lay in his lap
where it had always lain,
firm on his knees
with the weight of poems.
A thousand, and more,
each with a piece of him,
notes in the song
that had made him whole.
When he turned the pages
smooth under his palm,
his eyes glazed in snow,
the colour of the margin:
'More than bones to leave
behind. More than bones'.

Off Duty NZ

Off duty the sergeant dug his garden,
moved it every other month,
shrubs, plants, scoria river, clothes-line,
first in front then behind the house.
He dug all day unless it rained too hard
when likely he'd crouch under some broad tree
gumboots mulching deep
rather than go inside and paint the walls.
He coaxed leaves above his iron roof
whose corrugations rattled in the wind
and he watched the branches thicken,
his plot fenced in their bark.
The one gap was the concrete his drive made
and only his son who trundled after him
with his real rabbit and his rusty bike,
and his wife Ivy, stuck at the sink window
wondering where the garden'd moved again,
witnessed his labour.

                Manuka, paw paw
and totara came off his tongue
like third-form French when I called
sometimes and he led me through the rockery
to his latest variegated leaf.
It had been a long way,
but that was all over now
and mostly the seargent didn't speak much,
eyes flat upon the earth.
Once, though, when he lifted them to mine
I saw him say he knew how easy dying was,

how stupidly easy it was to die.
Or maybe I got it wrong
and he was just asking if there was anything else,
if there was anything else at all
before he turned to lock up his spades
neat as reports in a filing cabinet.

Koru

koru curl koru curl
you hold the world
koru curl koru curl
as your leaves unfurl

whirl and swirl
my green-eyed girl
twirl and whirl
my precious pearl

koru curl koru curl
all the seas turn
koru curl koru curl
foetal as your fern

Kaioraora

Hey, Maori
your face looks stupid
silly, vacant
without its moko.
Put your bloody make-up on,
Coco.

Haere mai, haere mai:
rub my nose.

Hey, Maori
you butcher our lingo
with all that spit.
Put your tongue away
you brainless shit.

Kati kati, kati kati:
kiss my arse.

Sonnet for Paul Gaugin

Tant de mystère dans tant de clarté
Stéphane Mallarmé

In Hiva Oa, coiled in mazarine,
god of the purple earth, great Tefaton,
lifts his larvaed forests to the sun
which spins a burning marzipan of dreams.
Below, a blaze of pinks and violets
flattens its lascivious tongue on virgin
flora, pandarus leaves where the lizards live
slipping their bellies on giant insects.
Quivering red wings of the chimera
hiding their brilliance away from harm
disturb the peacock's fabulous silence,
her feathers of emerald and sapphire
swooning in the breeze of coconut palms.
So much mystery in so much brightness!

Elixir of Te'amana

Te'amana, Te'amana
    come lie with me
Te'amana, Te'amana
    make me feel clean
Te'amana, Te'amana
    stretch out till dawn
Te'amana, Te'amana
    make me new born
Te'amana, Te'amana
    your silken hair
Te'amana, Te'amana
    will ease my care
Te'amana, Te'amana
    your mango breath
Te'amana, Te'amana
    will stave off death
Te'amana, Te'amana
    girl be mine
Te'amana, Te'amana
    my concubine

III

Photo

I took down your photo yesterday.
I was tired of its limboid beauty,
tired of the tales it told about you
and the temperatures of your body,
showing everything, knowing nothing.
You, there, on the Bank Holiday beach,
anxious, then as now, for an audience,
smiling, winking, blank at the shutter,
never knowing, in your rigid weather
and winds, when I would have you cry.
So I shut my eyes to the hard line
of your lips, and here on the mantelpiece
in my dark room tangled memories
develop the hairs of your absence.

Car

That ridiculous panting heap,
that subsiding shambles of limbs,
levers, seatbelts and pantyhose
hatchbacked in the mountain layby;
that pungency of soiled velour,
that exhaustion of springs, cassettes,
ashtrays, wrappings, that agony
of vanity mirrors, unbuttoned
glove compartments and treaded tongues
high in the mountain's misted glass:
what was it but a quick joyride
to the breaker's yard? What was it
but a collision of blood and bone
dipping in the moon's full beam?

Fantasy Physics

You proved it at the waterfall
that day we ventured out and found
a tufted privacy where all
the gaping woodland gathered round.
Dark pools in pools nobody'd swum
before your quantum breasts and braid,
silky aureoles proud and plumb
as acorns bobbing in the glade.
Breathless you turned when the mirror
tilted and light unlaced your thighs:
prismatic suns were caught in fir
where all the seven Severns rise.
Soon each colour found its level,
mining diamonds in your navel.

Tea

How did you feel afterwards
when they brought you a cup of tea
tidied your pillow and said
you could take it easy for a while?
Did you lie back wistfully,
the cup warm in your hands,
and measure that imperceptible hole
inside you
against the satisfaction
of having saved our freedom?
Did the nurse, if she was a nurse,
smile reassuringly, or did she look
through you
jealous of her white sheets,
slopping out mechanically
before she replenished the fridge?

And how do you feel now
when you lift a cup of tea to your lips
and think sometimes maybe about what
we nearly made? Doesn't that hole
inside you
get a little bigger every year,
a whole lot bigger in fact
so big you think it must be ready
to leave home at last and go looking
for its own freedom? Or is it
something you can't let go of,
that pulls harder than freedom
or love, or anything, sucking
at you
for the warmth
there in the emptiness as you start to sip?

Montage

A shaft of light in a gap of sawn-off
shops where the Grand once stood and hills dissolve
in a lantern of rain tumbling free-fall
like beer in a glass.
                    Say, who is shredding
my familiar clouds, making the grey gold?
Who is spooling rainbows through my dull eye
—hair, shoulders, lips in the loving darkness—
hoisting me on this perilous rake where
eddies of smoke swirl breathless as salmon?

Hair, shoulders, lips in the illumined dark
that opens spectacular as roses
on your fingertips when the cock crows loud
when searchlights cross in heaven
                        when latticed
sunshowers drench the regulation pine.

Llangwyryfon's Windmills

It's such a clear morning
I can see the blades on Llangwyryfon's windmills turning
and each rotation calibrates
the time your eyes once spent going round my face
watering these crevices:
Llangwyryfon, Llangwyryfon,
more than one spin, less than two,
which is the difference, I suppose, between modesty
and something else,
something I could never calibrate.

Llangwyryfon, Llangwyryfon,
I start to count to ease my pain.
Llangwyryfon, Llangwyryfon,
the blades turn and turn again.

24, 52, 100 times they slice the air
with morbid precision
and each rotation mutilates
the syllables of your name, the corners of your face
which I can hardly see or say:
Llangwyryfon, Llangwyryfon,
your lenten body drapes the pilon
incongruous above the village,
Llangwyryfon, Llangwyryfon,
chaste and bleeding, the death of time and hope for love.

Woman in a White Room

Sitting unseen on a white plastic chair,
pulling her sleeve and patting her hair,
she stares unseeing at the white marble floor,
one arch from Guernica, one from Miró.

Guardian of art treasures, mistress of time,
she knows no aesthetics, no thoughts sublime.
What to do for dinner? Who's got the rent?
Did he say 'Wednesday'? How was it meant?

She smiles sort of bored when children come in,
her isosceles corner trapping the din.
She stands up correctly, then walks round slow,
one arch from Guernica, one from Miró.

Reina Sofía, Madrid

Ciudad Rodrigo (1812-1994)

Proud against the monumental sky
your rough hewn turrets and feudal dome
climb above the Agueda where storks fly
and red-rag soldiers once dreamt of home.
Wounded by the senseless palindrome
of bell on clapper, clapper on bell,
the mind, too, migrates: a citadel
breached and burning on an icy night;
Picton, cursing, hoarse in cannon light:
'On, you thirsty scum! Aye, on to hell!'

Toledo

Only birds breathe in Toledo,
having no respect for the past.
The rest of us walk somnambular
down streets as tight as a nun's arse:
the Cathedral, bell-tower, junk shops,
stiff with swords, fonts, Count Orgaz.

But by the banks of the Tagus
where the *escudero* went for kicks,
where brown water laps plastic bags
beneath the Alcántara bridge,
a ghetto-blaster on the rocks
makes disco music for kids:

'Hey, Javi, you big pile of shit!'
'Mari, cunt-face, go suck your tit!'

Madrid–Soria

Soria fría, Soria pura,
cabeza de Extremadura . . . Antonio Machado

[Madrid, 9.40]
Bulldozers are busy making sky,
flattening the city's rubbish out
where new concrete towers will rise.

[Alcalá, 10.03]
A dozen backpackers erupt,
swearing, raving, and two kissing
so deep my lips begin to suck.

[Guadalajara, 10.21]
Pilons, sidings, backloads, frontloads;
cars stand at level crossings,
glide noiselessly down open roads.

[Sigüenza, 11.20]
A man strides the platform, handsome,
dapper; his wife the Moorish step
behind, a kid biting her thumb.

[Almazán, 12.15]
The poplars have yet to bud:
dry stone walls, decrepit farms,
ashen hills in stale, crusty lumps;

crumbling stone, cadmium earth, outcrops
of rock where a buzzard circles,
stunted trees, roofless walls, bald hilltops;

cement-coloured slopes, a sallow field;
rivers that flow to the Duero;
a harness and a buckler shield!
[Soria, 12.55]

Waiting for Goya

Sparrows
materializing on the rock
face, issuing from the conched
wall, as from a conjuror's
cloak, sallying into the Madrid
light, in multitudes,
each wing, beak, note
an Easter miracle.
Sparrows preening, chirping,
thirsting for the sparkling
light, darting from the living
rock, when a girl walks
out, her face against the lake
shimmering.

★

People swarm too
with the bland curiosity of tourists
as the day takes on its Sunday shape
in a languid rococo queue.
Goya was born
a round number of years ago
and we wait to walk through
walls where his miracles hang
in their own warm light, or
delve into a windowless room
where hags spoon soup, dogs
howl and witches float on stone
clouds, to wonder again why
a deaf man painted his walls black.

IV

Dog

He got to her finally,
when I was painting out the front.
His mind had been on nothing else
for two months, ever since
I bought the hutch and spent
a morning nailing two by twos
and wire mesh together
till it looked the part.
The girls' eyes popped and he watched,
snout wet against the glass,
as they cooed her, cuddled her, fed her.
'Strange', said one, 'Real rabbits
cost less than plastic'. 'He's jealous',
said the other, at the whine.

Two months' constant vigilance:
kitchen door, garden gate, hooked run.
Two months' supervised toiletry,
the combed lawn an exercise yard
for dog and rabbit in shifts.
But his time came when I was left
one heavy August day,
and my mind, dulled by radiospeak
and the brush's monotonous swish
swish, sank down the paintpot's thick
spiral so deep it barely told the Platters'
topmost note from a squeal
when his teeth found her furry neck.

Fred the Pole

Fred the Pole was a Latvian
refugee with his own teeth
and his own way of talking,
half Welsh, half something else.
He'd left his pit, walked across
Europe in a month and spent 35 years
in a fur factory watching Swansea
Town on Saturdays when Allchurch–
Medwin-Charles-Allchurch and Jones
was the forward line and a fat man called
Johnny King who died in South Africa
kept goal. 'One thing I can tell you'
said Fred through erratic teeth:
'Without that fat man they'd be in
the First Division now'.

                  Outside
the Vetch the piece of Wales Fred knew
best stood 3ft off the ground in
the Gorseinon & Loughor British Legion
which was once a mineowner's mansion.
7.30 every night Fred polished his boots,
razored his moustache and stepped
gingerly down Brynamlwg Rd
missing the dogshit and cracked pavements
till he reached the parquet floor of
the Gorseinon & Loughor British Legion
where he chalked FP on a piece of slate
sat down with his beer
and waited till the baize was his.
'One thing I can tell you', said Fred
the Pole lifting his glass and showing
his long teeth: 'This beer is piss'.

Cwmclettwr

for Mary and for John

Only young trees line the river in May,
slender ash, sapling oak, some small-leaved lime;
their green veins translucent, embryonic
as song that beats into a copper floor.
The water runs faster after the rain,
foaming on mossed shelvings and stepping-stones
where the sure-footed cross to an upturned
trunk, its gnarled roots pointing like foxes' snouts.
Clumps of fern, soft cranesbills, fading bluebells,
cracked bark, yellow lichen, a stray jackdaw,
and the sense of a world within one's reach.
A short walk for someone in a hurry,
for a girl with liquid eyes who loved trees
so much she hides behind them when you pass.

18.5.96

Ice-creams in Aberdaron

On reading R.S. Thomas' *Autobiographies*

The English are licking their ice-creams in Aberdaron.
In the church of Saint Hywyn an Anglican minister
kneels before his untenanted cross. What thoughts will enter
his head as he waits aching in the penumbra of stone?

An ash-tree, after frost, playing like a golden fountain;
the roar of jets overhead, drowning the voice of the sea?
The crease of a line on water that seeks the destiny
of fish; the ritual slaughter of vowels where Maelgwyn
bobbed like flotsam on the tide?

                    Peasants still wash their brutish
hands in Manafon's riverstone glass, streaking the miracle
of the bread and wine. A blackbird lifts his song in April,
light as Degas' flounces, rousing a converted cottage
that stands empty three parts of the year.

                    On the bough of Llŷn
the Milky Way guides new pilgrims like so many nightjars
from the African dark and by mid May more birds than stars
will nest in Eglwysfach, but must we ask what does it mean?

What does it mean, poet, that the meaning's in the waiting?
Are wonder and agony one? Can birds migrate but not
people? Say, firebrand, say, son of Glyndŵr or Ghandi, what
language do you pray in? Windsor Welsh? Why so much hating?

★

Yet you're right, you are right: it's not just ice-cream the English
lick in Aberdaron, nor is it lollies the Welsh suck.
Double-scoops with chocolate flake and walnut ripples on sticks
tempt mouths all the way down to Bardsey's foaming interstice.

And when, at last, the small congregation leaves Saint Hywyn,
and you listen to the air recomposing itself, what new
composure floods your mind as the stones regroup around you
and the waves crash hoarse as twenty thousand saints arguing?

I hear them too, on summer evenings, looking across
this bay at the Afallon of Llŷn, where the living and dead
meet in green corruscations, and I see you, on the edge
of paradise and hell, rivetted to that Celtic cross.

I see you, Mister No-one, where the tide laps your bible,
unravelling the parable of the good Samaritan,
heading home with two mackerel as dark falls in Aberdaron,
to gut on a hard board, pick clean on a narrow table.

Ron's Patch

In memory of Ron Berry

From Blaencwm to Ynysyfio
that's as far as I go.

From Blaenrhondda to Ynyswen
and back again.

If I was a peregrine
I'd nest on the Llyn.

If I could fly further
I'd hunt up in Merthyr.

But I'm a nuthatch
and I know my patch.

From Blaencwm to Ynysyfio
that's as far as I go.

From Blaenrhondda to Ynyswen
and back again.

The White Line

for Dick

The girl who wrote me a message once
in unjoined letters has died, someone said,
but in a voice so gentle I thought I'd dreamt it.
And back the images came in Indian file
bumping like kids I could do nothing with:

The white line that stretched across the yard
from the Gothic porch —a double porch, *Boys* up,
Girls down— to the stone canteen where cabbage
and semolina from the same vats was spooned
in different directions, *Girls* right, *Boys* left:
that white line went across the yard, up the steps,
into my brain.

The windows on the County bus
where we grew big on the top deck, smoking,
swearing, misting the glass to finger huge tits
and sweaty tools, singing *Never go to Heaven*,
In the Quartermaster's Store and stamping
Not Fade Away into the girls below: that bus went
up and down the valley in an impenetrable fog.

The dance-floor at the Boys' Club that we ringed
in shiny shoes, standing all night like flamingos
on one leg without setting foot on the chalk
where sec-mod teds moved with unseemly ease
and held or touched girls whose elbows, skirts
and pony-tails lifted in unfathomable unison:
that ring was the circus of my humiliations.

Paul Marshman's hands that he offered me
on the concrete pitch one break time, palms
cupped, fingers interlocked, inviting me,
within sight of the girls' railings, to insert
a digit or two before turning triumphant
and howling incomprehensibly: that gobbed
mit was the sewer of my mottled dreams.

Fresh as paint on my forehead, that line
we never crossed, that white line our eyes
wouldn't cross when a ball strayed and a hand
attached to a limb belonging to an unseen
torso threw it back from a world where the girl
who wrote me a message once in unjoined
letters lived and breathed and perhaps wondered

why, next time we met, I could hardly speak,
why we spent our whole lives in a concrete yard
with a white line and a double porch, *Boys* up,
Girls down.

            For the kiss we never savoured,
for the years spent loving ghosts, for the message
you sent, know, at least, I see you skipping still.
And the answer is yes, always yes, yes.

Half-Closing

It's Thursday, half-closing . . . and the Basin
is deluged with a slow, spillaging mist.
My father, at the lounge window, his eyes
quick and green, vaulting treetops in the park
opposite, anxious for a chink of light.
My father, at the clock, at the window,
now on tiptoe, neck craned, hands cupped, eyebrows
arched to heaven like two El Greco saints
-one Hope, one Resignation- doodling
the same indecipherable tune. Thursday,
the shop shut; my father, at the window,
desperate for a sign that his life's his own,
before the weather closes in for good:
'Anne, Anne, I think it's going to clear up'.

Il Gigante Buono

for John Charles

Such a small country
made such a big man?
When you ran out the tunnel
John
the pitch was like a stamp,
Wales an Amazon.

Worth your weight in gold
to merchants of Juventus,
you never sold us short
John,
mud all over your bonny face,
the red vest on.

Eschatological Reminiscences in the Rain

The tips have gone.

And so have Ryan's lorries that moved like ants on uneven ground
humping the still partly edible carcasses of other insects to secret
places where their bones'd be picked nearly clean then dumped
with fingernail shavings under the eyes of nocturnal scavengers
who'd come out to find one last globule to suck on or be sucked by.

The tips have all gone.

And so has the boy who woke up in a strange bedroom in Cardiff
where he'd slept uneasily for six months and looked out his window
one morning at the nothing but grey sky that pressed on wet slate
like a shroud with not a curve of earth or blade of grass to be seen
and who felt such a hole in his gut he wanted to vomit.

All the tips have gone now.

And so has the man who came back once on a Kawasaki from the vast
skies of Calgary Alberta where the whiteness is almost permanent and
the air has ten pigmentations of purity only to be confronted by armies
of pines and artificially sown grass that lies as smooth-sided in places as
a billiard table and who was indignant enough to say:

It's like they never lived.

Home

I came home to the snow
and saw the mountain big
and beautiful, dressed to kill,
bumps dazzling like a Persil ad,
the black river and trees draining it
of scum, the clouds an off-white blouse
of some unfortunate child.
I came home to the snow
and saw the mountain's jigsaw grow,
knowing where its colours were.

Welsh Clouds

It was a good day for clouds:
one half of the sky deep blue
the other half puffed up in a snowy steeplechase,
but softer/whiter than the snows far off on Plynlimon,
silvery in the Powys shallows.

And sat in my sun on Penglais Hill
watching polar camels/koala bears unfold their slow-motion plot
in the lumpy, bumpy amphitheatre above me (the sea to my right
a golf-course lake, and Llŷn, on its camber, beads of islands) my first
thought was of poets who'd seen them before
—lonely-cloud/torn-cloud/both-sides-now poets—
and I felt a kind of practiced awe.

Looking again at the blanched mushrooms that climb
in cherubic limbs to the talcumed top of the sky
it occurred to me:
this
nebular curve south
exactly/unmistakably
matches the auriculate sweep of Cardigan Bay
—five miles in and five miles high—
and it's as if Wales, or most of it, is up in the sky
like a map on a page
waiting to be read.

I keep looking
unable to tell if my rumpled cottager's bed
is being made or unmade,
if the question dripping from the cone of Llŷn
/serrated vinegar-stained chipbags to the south
—'What is a Welshman?'/'When was Wales?'—
isn't provocatively in the wrong person/alliteratively in the wrong tense.

Watching clouds
it's easy to subside into diaspora/be seduced
by the languor of entropy,
but in that feeling of utter dissipation
with its myriad tiny explosions/unseparated microseconds of release
you sense a momentum that evolves of its own
that won't be held
to a page/map/mind.
And look: the stain of a new cloud moves on the Irish Sea.